GREAT WHITE SHARK

Madeline Nixon

www.av2books.com

Step 1
Go to **www.av2books.com**

Step 2
Enter this unique code
BSZECOSXQ

Step 3
Explore your interactive eBook!

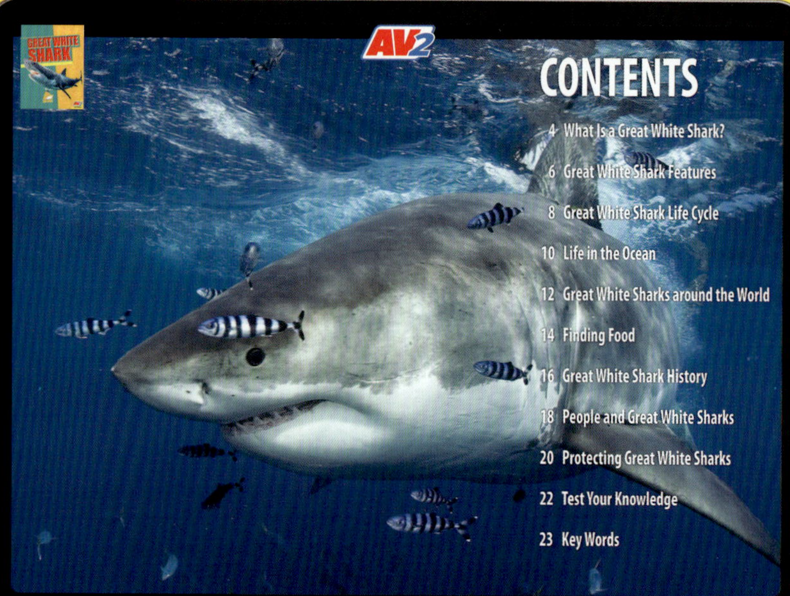

AV2 is optimized for use on any device

Your interactive eBook comes with...

Contents
Browse a live contents page to easily navigate through resources

Audio
Listen to sections of the book read aloud

Videos
Watch informative video clips

Weblinks
Gain additional information for research

Try This!
Complete activities and hands-on experiments

Key Words
Study vocabulary, and complete a matching word activity

Quizzes
Test your knowledge

Slideshows
View images and captions

... and much, much more!

CONTENTS

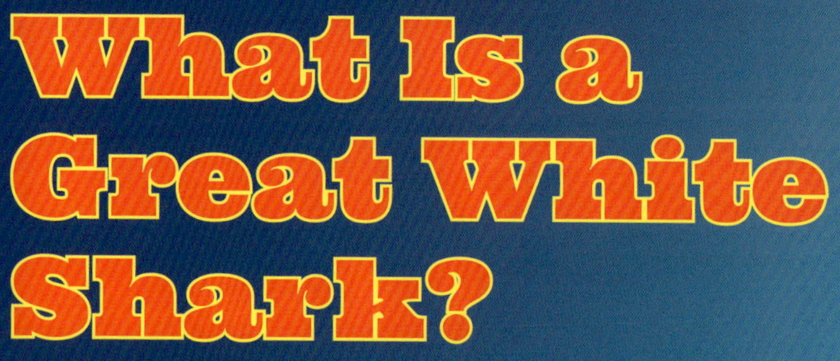

What Is a Great White Shark?

Great white sharks get their name from their white bellies. They are some of the biggest **predators** in the ocean. They are long and fast. That makes them dangerous hunters. Unlike many other fish, sharks have eyelids to protect their eyes. The great white shark even has a clear third eyelid. This lets it see while its eyes are protected.

"Unlike most fish, white sharks are intelligent, highly inquisitive creatures."

—Alison Kock, Marine Biologist

Great White Shark

Scientific Name *Carcharodon carcharias*

Diet Carnivore

Size 15–20 feet (4.6–6.1 meters)

Weight More than 2.5 tons (2.3 metric tons)

Conservation Status Vulnerable

Population Less than 3,500

Great White Shark Features

Great white sharks have many features. Some help them to hunt and feed. Others help them to swim quickly.

Tail
A great white shark has a large and strong tail fin. This fin helps it swim at top speed.

Skin

A great white shark is gray on top. This allows it to match the ocean floor. That way, it can hide from **prey** when hunting.

Blood

A great white shark has warm blood. This helps it to live in both warm and cold waters.

Great White Shark Life Cycle

A female great white shark has babies every two to three years. She is pregnant for about a year. The shark pups hatch from eggs inside their mother. They eat **unfertilized** eggs until they are born. At birth, they weigh about 50 to 60 pounds (22.6 to 27.2 kg). They are about 3 to 5 feet (91.4 to 152.4 centimeters) long. Great white sharks can live up to 70 years.

How Big Are Sharks?

Female great white sharks are bigger than males.

Human
5.5 feet (1.7 m)

Blacktip Shark
8 feet (2.4 m)

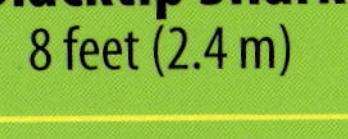

Bull Shark
11.5 feet (3.5 m)

Shortfin Mako Shark
12 feet (3.7 m)

Tiger Shark
16 feet (4.9 m)

Great Hammerhead Shark
20 feet (6.1 m)

Great White Shark
20 feet (6.1 m)

Whale Shark
32 feet (9.8 m)

Life in the Ocean

Great white sharks can control their body temperature. This is called **endothermy**. It lets these fish live in many different places.

Great white sharks can be found off coastlines and in the middle of the ocean. They swim near the **surface** of the water. This is where they usually hunt. They can also dive as deep as 4,265 feet (1,300 m). Great white sharks do not stay in one place. They **migrate** several times during their lives.

SHARK BITES
Great white sharks can jump 8–10 feet (2.4–3 m) out of the water.

Great White Sharks around the World

Great white sharks can be spotted in warm and cool **salt water** around the world. They are found almost everywhere except in the freezing waters near Antarctica and the far north.

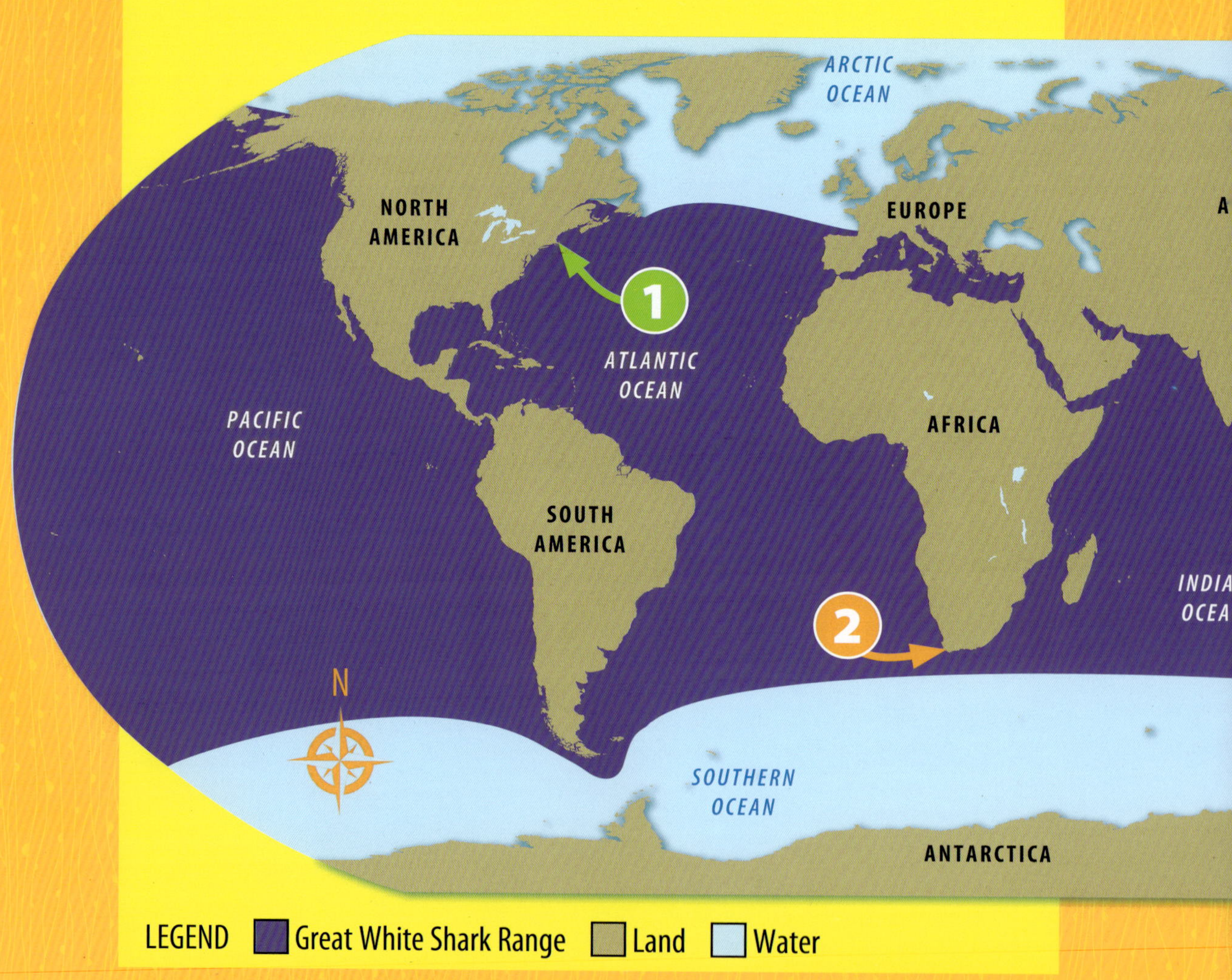

1 Cape Cod, United States

Scientists believe that the waters near Cape Cod act as a **nursery** for great white sharks.

2 Dyer Island, South Africa

Many great white sharks live in the waters near Dyer Island. That is because there are many penguins and seals to eat. This area is nicknamed "shark alley."

PACIFIC OCEAN

AUSTRALIA 3

3 Stewart Island, New Zealand

There are many great white sharks near New Zealand. They are protected in this country.

Finding Food

Great white sharks are **carnivores**. This means that they eat only meat. They eat dolphins, seals, penguins, rays, and turtles. They also sometimes eat other sharks.

Great white sharks sneak up on prey from below. Then, their **torpedo** shape and strong fins help them swim quickly to the top of the water. The great white shark's scientific name means "ragged-toothed." Their jagged teeth help them tear food apart.

SHARK BITES
A great white shark can have more than 300 teeth. Each jaw has between 5 and 15 rows of teeth.

Great White Shark History

Great white sharks were discovered in 1758. However, scientists believe they have been around since the time of dinosaurs. Today, great white sharks are at the top of the **food chain**. Orcas are their only predators.

There have been many different names for great white sharks, including "white pointers."

People and Great White Sharks

Up to half of all shark bites on humans are caused by great white sharks. They bite things to find out if they are food. This is called sample-biting. Most sample bites do not kill people. The shark realizes the person is not its normal food and leaves. However, great whites are still some of the most dangerous sharks to people.

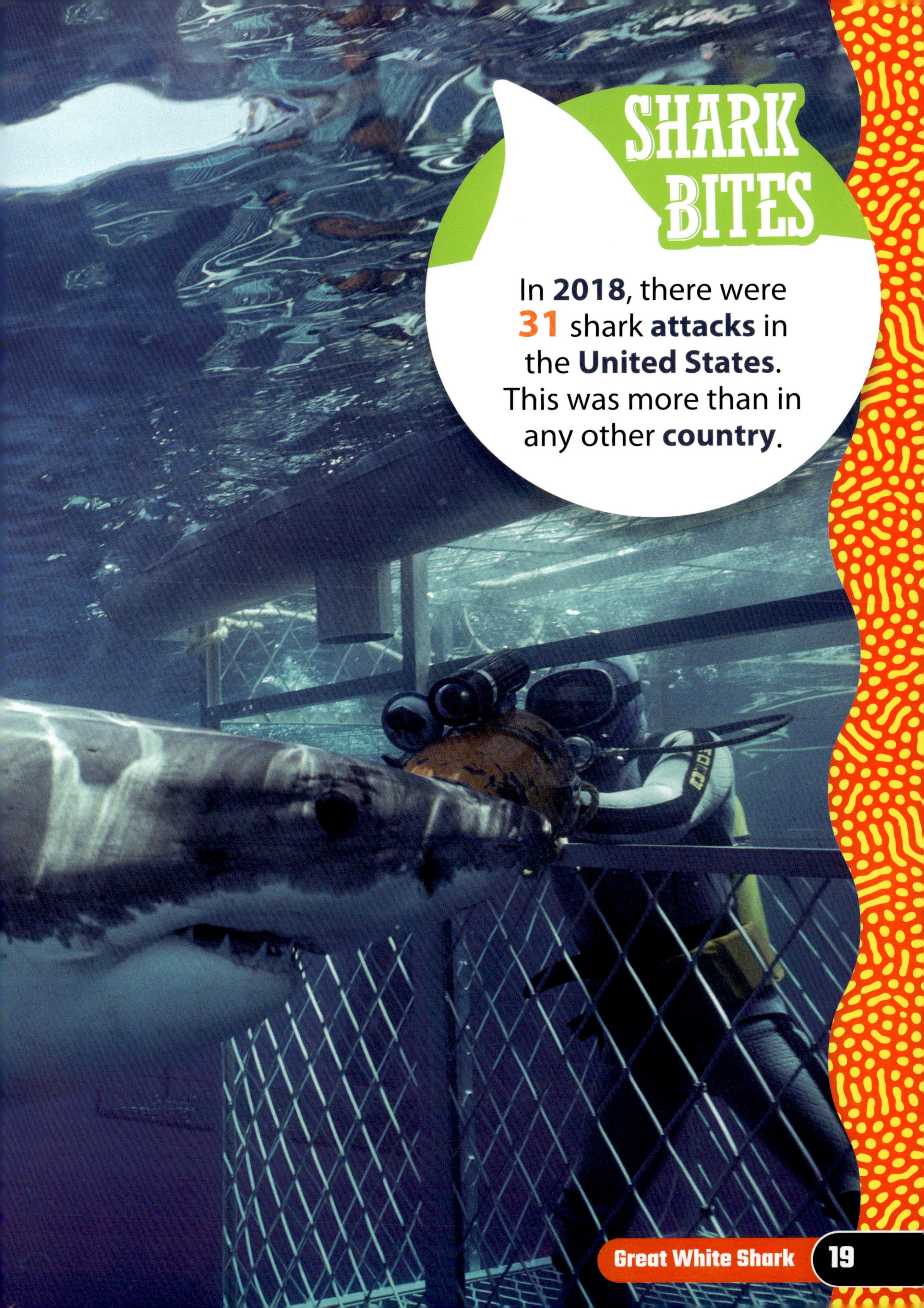

SHARK BITES

In **2018**, there were **31** shark **attacks** in the **United States**. This was more than in any other **country**.

Great white sharks have been protected in American waters since 1997.

Protecting Great White Sharks

Great white sharks face threats from humans. Bites from these sharks cause fear and anger. However, this also leads to shark deaths. Great white sharks are killed for trophies. They are also hunted for their fins and meat.

Great white sharks are in danger. Few places around the world have laws protecting them. South Africa, Australia, New Zealand, and the United States are some of the few countries that do. These countries have many great white sharks.

Great White Shark Conservation Status

Extinct

Extinct in the Wild

Critically Endangered

Endangered

Vulnerable

Near Threatened

Least Concern

Test Your Knowledge

1
When were great white sharks discovered?

1758

2
Which countries have laws protecting great white sharks?

South Africa, Australia, United States, and New Zealand

3
What are the only ocean predators of great white sharks?

Orcas

4
What does a great white shark's gray back help it do?

Blend into the bottom of the ocean

5
What does a great white shark's scientific name mean?

"Ragged-toothed"

6
Where do great white sharks get their name?

From their white bellies

7
Why can great white sharks live in both warm and cool waters?

They are warm-blooded

8
What location is nicknamed "shark alley"?

Dyer Island, South Africa

Key Words

carnivores: animals that eat meat

endothermy: the ability to control body temperature

food chain: a way of organizing living things where animals at the top eat those below them

migrate: to move from one place to another

nursery: where young are born and raised

predators: animals that hunt other animals

prey: an animal that is hunted by another

salt water: water that is salty, like the ocean

surface: the top of a body of water

torpedo: a long, oval-shaped missile that travels in water

unfertilized: an egg that will not grow into an animal

Index

Get the best of both worlds.

AV2 bridges the gap between print and digital.

The expandable resources toolbar enables quick access to content including **videos**, **audio**, **activities**, **weblinks**, **slideshows**, **quizzes**, and **key words**.

Animated videos make static images come alive.

Resource icons on each page help readers to further **explore key concepts**.

Published by AV2
350 5th Avenue, 59th Floor
New York, NY 10118
Website: www.av2books.com

Library of Congress Control Number: 2019955127

ISBN 978-1-7911-2107-5 (hardcover)
ISBN 978-1-7911-2108-2 (softcover)
ISBN 978-1-7911-2109-9 (multi-user eBook)
ISBN 978-1-7911-2110-5 (single-user eBook)

Printed in Guangzhou, China
1 2 3 4 5 6 7 8 9 0 24 23 22 21 20

022020
101119

Project Coordinator: John Willis
Designer: Terry Paulhus

Every reasonable effort has been made to trace ownership and to obtain permission to reprint copyright material. The publishers would be pleased to have any errors or omissions brought to their attention so that they may be corrected in subsequent printings.

AV2 acknowledges Alamy, Getty Images, Minden Pictures, and Shutterstock as its primary image suppliers for this title.